Mama's Blues

poems by

Albert DeGenova

Finishing Line Press
Georgetown, Kentucky

Mama's Blues

Copyright © 2022 by Albert DeGenova
ISBN 978-1-64662-938-1 First Edition
All rights reserved under International and Pan-American Copyright Conventions. No part of this book may be reproduced in any manner whatsoever without written permission from the publisher, except in the case of brief quotations embodied in critical articles and reviews.

ACKNOWLEDGMENTS

"Mama's Blues," *After Hours*, Issue #3/Winter 2001
"The Bus Stop," *A Good Hammer*, Albert DeGenova, Timberline Press, 2014.
"First Love" (Part I from the "First Love" series), *No More Can Fit Into an Evening* anthology, Four Windows Press, 2020.
"To Earth Softly Settles" and "White Flag" (Part VII and Part X, respectively, from the "First Love" series), *Storms of the Inland Sea: Poems of Alzheimer's and Dementia Caregiving* anthology, The Chrysalis Project, 2021.

Publisher: Leah Huete de Maines
Editor: Christen Kincaid
Cover Art: Santiago Weksler
Author Photo: Cole DeGenova
Cover Design: Elizabeth Maines McCleavy

Order online: www.finishinglinepress.com
also available on amazon.com

Author inquiries and mail orders:
Finishing Line Press
PO Box 1626
Georgetown, Kentucky 40324
USA

Table of Contents

The Bus Stop 1

Mama's Blues 2

Osterizer Chocolate Shake 3

First Love 4

Ghost 18

Spring Again 19

Dedicated to my Mom
Donata "Donna" Dydo

Look a here, Bill, I'd come to you one day
I was tryin' to make a way
And you was cryin' and you told me
One day you would tell me who you were cryin' for.
Who were you cryin' for?

Mama, yeah.
What did you want with your mama?
A drink of water, Mama.
Well, go ahead and tell me how Mama treated you.

—Lightnin' Hopkins, lyric "Mama Blues"

The Bus Stop

Here I stood under an umbrella watching water flow along the curb like racing rapids—where on winter mornings I waited wrapped in scarves and down coat and hat pulled down tight over my ears and forehead only my nose and eyes exposed to the wind, nose running, my young thin moustache frozen—where I stood waiting for the Archer Ave bus that would take me from 55th Street on Chicago's southwest side first to California Ave. and grammar school, then to Throop Street and high school, then all the way into "the Loop" for college. The corner at Archer Ave and 55th where I hung out with my rock band buddies at Chicken LaBelle drinking cokes and eating fries joking with the owner Joe Arkelian and flirting with his daughters; next door Pisa Pizza, where my sister hung out, we would order gravy bread, crusty Italian bread dipped in red sauce, 50 cents; across the street, Jack-In-The-Box where we ate tacos for the first time, where Laura Schnear, that beauty with huge brown eyes and pouting lips, hung out with her pot-head friends; the grassy triangle space we called "the Hill" that filled the angle of Archer as it met 55th where all the long-haired "freaks" hung out and we "greasers" wouldn't dare. This is the bus stop where I saw Gina DiDomenico every morning, a girl from our "gang" and Chicken La Belle, eventually asked her to go to a party with me, for months after that we necked in the backseat of the bus we called the "green limousine," went to my prom, got married three years later still riding the bus, me still in college, she on her way to work in the credit office at Wieboldt's department store.

Years earlier, my mother waited on the same corner, met my father on the Archer bus, he would get on at Lockwood Ave, they'd ride downtown together—Mom was a ticket girl at the Chicago Theatre, Dad worked at the Palmer House Hotel.

They divorced too.

Mama's Blues

They say the blues
is a good woman feelin' bad,
      feelin' bad.
I inherited the blues from my mother.

Sitting at the kitchen table
tearing tissue into little white crumbs
that would never dry a tear, not anymore,
      not anymore.
She sang the blues, sang the blues
about hating him for giving me his name—
and maybe this time a hooker would shoot him
instead of stealing his Cadillac.

The blues was the pink robe she wrapped around her pajamas
making my lunch and searching his pockets for bus fare.
The blues followed her into dusty corners
but couldn't be scrubbed away
      though she tried, she tried.
It waited behind the sofa that became her bed,
      became her narrow bed.

Her blues is in me like a nursery rhyme
      that echoes
when I see those sad eyes
      all those sad eyes
of good women feelin' bad.

Her face, my mother's face
lit by the all-night TV
is the blues
still calling to me, still begging me
      Don't be that name,
            Don't   be that name.

Osterizer Chocolate Shake

My mother is the first to call
on my 50th birthday.
In three months she will be 70
and we decide together
there will be no more birthday parties.
We will stay 50 and 70 forever
aging under our woolen sweaters, no more silly candles.
We've grown up together
she's always said,
and now, after Sunday dinners,
we take our blood pressure
together, a kind-of competition.

On my 50th birthday, after my mother's call,
from the corner cabinet over my refrigerator
I pull down the green Osterizer.
It wears the same orange dustcover that it
wore the day my mother gave it to me,
25 years ago, helping me to setup my new apartment—
me broke and recently divorced,
she had plenty of hand-me-downs.

I scoop in vanilla ice cream
add milk and plenty of
Hershey's syrup, push the "blend" button
the whir becoming chocolate shake
just like a first breath.

First Love

i.

You, who loved me first,
gave me words. Now,
I offer them back.
You forget
sometimes, so I
complete your sentence.
You were nineteen-years-old
counting my toes, your firstborn—
we've grown up together.
I was in the backseat as you
learned to drive. With no one
on my sidelines, you sent
my uncles.
        Today, at 57,
I have friends your age. Time,
that elastic measure
so much living between us,
your life, my life—the slant rhymes
I've left out. We've an unheard language.
No need to read your yellowing journals,
the passions you couldn't say out loud—
I understand, and maybe
our living is enough, you
just a few steps ahead, reaching back
to take my hand.
Look both ways you say again and again.
You, who I loved first,
to the last word.

ii.

Is it twenty after,
twenty 'til, I want to help
with the clock, those tricky slight-of-
hands, the face of missing numbers
where are the 10 and 11
in your bedroom of mementos
52 or 3, or 60 years ago
the incidental photos
a tape-cornered box at the back of a closet
stored away
Grandma's basement,
the parties, the food
the faces
the ballet of young days
in black & white,
the faded Polaroids—
the "Dance of the Sugarplum Fairy"
twirling in and out of
focus—what time shall we call this,
this clockless waning.

iii.

She's swallowed her diamonds
those prayers of youth, those pills
with no effect. I'm frying pork chops
exactly as I learned by watching her—
those careful dips in eggs and
breadcrumbs. Her Christmas cookies
don't taste the same, salt added twice,
one too many eggs. She asks,
Do I like cheese on my White Castle?
A precious crystal wine glass
I wash and dry carefully, away from the harsh
crusted frying pan. She reads
today's *Tribune*, relates a story without
moving her lips. She is happy
on my birthday. The ghost of a smile.
The smile of a ghost.

iv.

The slideshow
is my role
she must be
in every photo
this is her
birthday celebration
she was there, the witness
to sacraments and babies
and Sunday dinners in
her mother's basement
80 years of hair styles
clothes and men
and children's children
so many photos, so often
I was the photographer
how absent
the camera lets you be
but now she's 80 and I am 60
and her life is at my fingertips
in her eyes
her unspoken
off-stage legacy,
                what
what are you saying to me
rare
for her to be at the center
of the picture
never clowning, never
mugging for the camera,
each quiet smile through the lens
marked with another
distant Christmas
                what

were you saying to me
try louder now try
               please Mom
what do you want me to know

v.

There remains a
                diminished light
a motionless staring, searching the carpet for lost earrings
she goes gently into her dark night

wearing lipstick for her lost white knight
there's a reflex called yearning
what remains is distant sinking light.

Lost in the mirror, her face an ashen white
no toothpaste on the brush she's using
she goes slowly and confused into her dark night

surrounded by memories lost in flight
circling her bed in spirals descending
what remains is a faltering light.

But there remain undefined delights
a mysterious mother-instinct like loving
she carries gently into her dark night.

When she stares stony, no knowing fight,
is she wistfully musing
What remains of that
                setting light?
She slips sadly into her long dark night.

vi.

Her Mona Lisa smile
bruised now with broken words
and thin kisses pressed tight
against the bite of empty time,
she wants to know her place
at this round table without chairs—
she grasps my elbow
    ring around the rosie
we all fall down.

vii.

She runs, away, like a wind
that shakes the shutters
   I've got to go   rattles
the heart of her daughter
who folds her white cane
into impotent, infinite chase
and cries and tries,
and cries again, *Wait! Mom! Wait!*

Mom runs like a wind
unmoored,
unleashed on an ocean of sails—
her outstretched arms
those broken booms, the jibs
of fear, free and falling
a wind like a breath to earth softly settles
the wordless tempest withering within.

I couldn't stop, she tells her daughter
like apology, like admission,
like loss, but more
like disaster.

viii.

Every week we go out for our Tuesday dinner date. This week it's Mexican food, you enjoy Tacos Al Pastor. You know this. This week, I gently redirect your spoon, the salsa bowl is not soup. I know it's an easy mistake. I chatter the same stories as last week.

I ask you to wait. I go to the counter to pay. I'm steps away. You take the green hot sauce—easy pour, tapered-tip open nozzle. Stop! No! You can't drink that!

You can't

ix.
failing the questions to be answered at Aspired Living of Westmont, Illinois

If only
on my 50th birthday and
she about to turn 70, (we promised
no more birthdays!) I'd asked back then
all the important questions.
Her favorite color?
I know, I'm pretty sure
it's blue,
she wore blue so often—

and food? Tomatoes
her garden overflowed,
August red-heavy on vines,
she really likes tomatoes.
So thick, her sauce for Sunday dinners!

Favorite season? I think,
is Spring
her birthday is in May,
she has always loved
Easter Lilies. Though I
love Fall, and we've agreed
on so much. Her song with my father
was "Autumn Leaves."

Music?
Oh Yes, music too!
makes her tap rhythms on her lap
as we drive for our pizza dinner,
Pavarotti's Neapolitan love songs spinning in
her ears—aren't they, shouldn't they?

When she tells my son
I don't want to make you sad
she knows she can't say his name,
when she insists
on standing in the door
to watch me leave, to wave
just as she did when my sons were babies,
I believe, she is remembering.
This is a verb in past tense.
How did she learn to dance?
The answers are hers—
mine, the circumstantial evidence.

x.

And now I pretend
to pray—
my secret mourning,
secret even from myself.
Too soon to cry, she's still
smiling at me, still
finding the rhythm in Louis Prima,
still my mom.
Do I pray because I should have cried
sooner? I pray like a child
as if making a wish, as if tears
would be my surrender
to the wheelchair, her swollen hands,
the odd twist in her smile.
Mine is an ambiguous white flag
I raise for me, for her
when she waves goodbye.

xi.
for the memorial service

I remember you with the hymnal
yours the soprano voice
ringing out above the congregation
but today there are no words to my song
no words to name the unknowable
god or death, or the answers
to questions I used to ask
How do you feel?
What did you eat for breakfast?
I sing along with one of your DVDs—
Do a deer a female deer,
Re, Mi, Fa, Sol, La, Ti
and I'm waiting for resolution
the scale at its end
that last note wants to move,
to lead to you, I hear your voice
in the neatly folded pajama top
at the top of the laundry basket,
in the Mediterranean cookbook
I read with my wife, your voice
hitting that *Do*, the tonic
loud and clear, resolved
and then
an octave higher
just like Julie Andrews
just like church.

xii.

On the roof the fiddler
(in the pot the red sauce
simmering down the hours)
plays perilous
these precious
bits and broken crystal wine glasses—
so quickly snow becomes stream
sunrise never repeats itself
this precarious
continuum
of traditions
her birthday gift to me
your favorite, steak parmesan—
wind and mountains instead
this year
(the red sauce tastes
less than)
my first year on the roof
neglecting my secret
dream ballrooms
so much is disrepair
this dear darkening
continuum
struggling for balance
as the sun
sets

Ghost

She crashed into my dream
like a train whistle blasting
through a crossing
I can feel
the heaving breath of
freight cars passing, going
somewhere into the blackness
at 3 am—
always something sinister
on that train—
what more does she want
windows rattle
I pull up the sheets, she
is not with me here
my dark night

Spring Again
> *after William Carlos Williams' "Spring and All"*
> *and with a nod to Federico Garcia Lorca*

Spring again, the year after
my mother dies

blood blooms into roses
roses bloom into blood
blooms into blood roses
into blooms roses blood

surviving this winter, this spring
of coughing, she couldn't have

I am here, the memories
imprison,
      the present
a prison

…Still the profound change
has come upon them, rooted they
grip down and begin to awaken.

Albert DeGenova is an award-winning poet, publisher, and teacher. He is the author of four books of poetry and two chapbooks. His last book, *Black Pearl: poems of love, sex and regret* was published by Purple Flag Press (an imprint of Virtual Artists Collective) in 2016. In 2018, Redbee Editions (an imprint of Argus House Press) released a second expanded edition of *Postcards to Jack*, DeGenova's collection of haibun and poetry. His work has also appeared in numerous anthologies and journals including: *RHINO, The Paterson Literary Review, Haibun Today, The Louisville Review, Pure Slush, Aesthetica Magazine, The Café Review, The Northampton Poetry Review*, and others. DeGenova is the founder, publisher and co-editor of *After Hours*, a journal of Chicago writing and art; the journal launched in June 2000. He received his MFA in Writing from Spalding University, Louisville, and leads several writing workshops throughout the year including an annual writing week at The Clearing Folk School in Ellison Bay, WI. He co-hosts the monthly Traveling Mollys reading series (virtual and in-person in Oak Park, IL) which is now in its 23rd year. He is also a blues saxophonist and one-time contributing editor to *Down Beat* magazine. DeGenova splits his time between Sturgeon Bay, WI, and the metro Chicago area.

www.ingramcontent.com/pod-product-compliance
Lightning Source LLC
LaVergne TN
LVHW041522070426
835507LV00012B/1752